# Table of Contents

1. Identify Your Skills and Interests..................................................................2
2. Freelancing ..........................................................................................5
3. Content Creation   10
4. Online Tutoring ..................................................................................14
5. Sell Products Online ..........................................................................18
6. Affiliate Marketing ............................................................................23
7. Online Surveys and Market Research ................................................26
8. Virtual Assistant ................................................................................30
9. Create an Online Course ..................................................................34
10. Freelance Writing ............................................................................38

# 1. Identify Your Skills and Interests

Start by assessing what skills you have or what you're interested in. This could be anything from writing, graphic design, programming, social media management, to online tutoring, and much more.

## Self-Assessment:

Take some time to reflect on your strengths, experiences, and hobbies.

Consider the tasks or activities that you enjoy doing and excel at.

Think about any specific skills you've developed through education, work, or personal interests.

These could be technical skills like programming or graphic design, soft skills like communication or organization, or domain-specific knowledge in areas like finance, health, or marketing.

## Skills Inventory:

Make a list of all the skills you possess, both hard and soft skills.

This could include technical skills such as coding languages, design software proficiency, writing proficiency, or any other skills relevant to the online marketplace.

Don't overlook soft skills like communication, problem-solving, time management, and creativity.

These are often just as valuable in the online marketplace.

## Interest Exploration:

Explore your interests and passions. What topics or activities do you find yourself naturally drawn to? What could you spend hours doing without feeling bored?

Consider hobbies, subjects you enjoy learning about, or topics you're passionate about.

Your interests can serve as a guide for finding online opportunities that align with your passions.

## Research Potential Opportunities:

Once you have a clear understanding of your skills and interests, research potential online opportunities that match them. For example:

If you're skilled at writing and passionate about health and fitness, you could explore freelance writing opportunities in the health and wellness niche.

If you have graphic design skills and an interest in fashion, you could create and sell custom-designed merchandise on platforms like Etsy or Redbubble.

If you're proficient in programming and interested in technology, you could offer web development services or create and sell software applications.

If you're a good communicator and enjoy interacting with people, you could explore online tutoring or virtual assistant roles.

If you're passionate about a specific topic or hobby, consider creating content (blogs, videos, podcasts) around that topic and monetizing it through advertising, sponsorships, or affiliate marketing.

## Evaluate Demand and Market Opportunities:

Research the demand for the skills and services you possess. Look for online job postings, freelance opportunities, or marketplaces related to your skills and interests.

Consider factors such as competition, market trends, and the potential for growth and profitability in your chosen niche.

Keep in mind that some niches may be more saturated than others, so it's important to find a balance between your interests and market demand.

By thoroughly assessing your skills and interests, you can better align yourself with online opportunities that not only have the potential to generate income but also bring you fulfillment and satisfaction.

The online marketplace is diverse, and there are numerous ways to leverage your skills and passions to make money online.

# 2. Freelancing

Platforms like Upwork, Freelancer, Fiverr, and PeoplePerHour allow you to offer your services to clients globally.

Create a profile highlighting your skills and start bidding on relevant projects.

**Choose Your Platform:**

Research and choose a freelancing platform that best fits your skills, interests, and goals.

Each platform has its own set of features, pricing structures, and user demographics.

Consider factors such as the types of projects available, competition level, fee structure, and user reviews.

**Create a Profile:**

Sign up for an account on your chosen freelancing platform.

Complete your profile with accurate and compelling information about yourself, your skills, and your experience. Your profile serves as your online resume and portfolio, so make sure to highlight your strengths and achievements.

Upload a professional photo and write a concise yet engaging bio that showcases your expertise and personality.

Include relevant samples of your work, such as portfolio items, previous projects, or links to your website or online portfolio.

Specify the services you offer, your rates, and your availability.

## Define Your Niche:

Identify your niche or specialization within your broader skill set. This could be based on industry, type of service, or specific expertise.

Specializing in a niche can help you stand out from the competition and attract clients who are looking for your particular skills and expertise.

Focus on developing and showcasing your expertise in your chosen niche through your profile, portfolio, and marketing efforts.

## Search for Projects:

Use the platform's search and filtering options to find projects that match your skills, interests, and availability.

Read project descriptions carefully and assess whether you're a good fit for the job based on your expertise and the client's requirements.

Pay attention to client reviews, ratings, and project budgets to gauge the credibility and suitability of potential clients.

## Submit Proposals:

Write personalized and tailored proposals for each project you're interested in. Address the client's specific needs and requirements, and explain how your skills and experience make you the best candidate for the job.

Highlight relevant examples of your past work or achievements that demonstrate your ability to deliver results.

Be concise, professional, and persuasive in your proposals, and avoid generic or copy-pasted responses.

## Communicate Effectively:

Once you've been hired for a project, communicate clearly and regularly with the client to ensure you understand their expectations and requirements.

Clarify any uncertainties or questions you have about the project upfront to avoid misunderstandings later on.

Keep the client updated on your progress, milestones, and any issues or challenges you encounter along the way.

Respond promptly to messages and inquiries from the client to demonstrate your professionalism and commitment to delivering high-quality work.

**Deliver High-Quality Work:**

Focus on delivering work that meets or exceeds the client's expectations and requirements.

Pay attention to detail, adhere to deadlines, and strive for excellence in every aspect of your work.

Be open to constructive feedback and willing to make revisions or adjustments as needed to ensure client satisfaction.

Aim to build long-term relationships with clients by consistently delivering exceptional results and providing outstanding customer service.

**Build Your Reputation and Portfolio:**

As you complete projects and receive positive feedback from clients, your reputation and credibility on the platform will grow.

Encourage satisfied clients to leave reviews and ratings on your profile to attract more clients in the future.

Continuously update your portfolio with new work samples and projects to showcase your skills and expertise to potential clients.

Stay active and engaged on the platform by participating in discussions, joining relevant groups or communities, and networking with other freelancers and clients.

## Manage Your Finances:

Keep track of your earnings, expenses, and taxes associated with freelancing.

Set aside a portion of your income for taxes and other business-related expenses.

Consider using accounting software or hiring a professional accountant to help you manage your finances effectively.

## Continuously Improve and Adapt:

Stay informed about industry trends, tools, and best practices related to your field of expertise.

Invest in ongoing learning and skill development to stay competitive in the freelancing marketplace.

Be adaptable and flexible in your approach, and be willing to pivot or adjust your strategies based on changes in the market or client needs.

By following these steps and staying committed to delivering high-quality work and exceptional customer service, you can build a successful freelancing career and generate a sustainable income online.

# 3. Content Creation

If you're good at writing, creating videos, or producing other forms of content, you can monetize it through platforms like YouTube, Medium, or blogging platforms. Once you build an audience, you can earn money through advertising, sponsorships, or affiliate marketing.

**Choose Your Platform:**

Select a platform that aligns with the type of content you want to create and your target audience. YouTube is ideal for video content, Medium is suitable for written articles and essays, and blogging platforms like WordPress or Blogger are great for hosting your own blog.

Consider factors such as the platform's audience size, demographics, content policies, monetization options, and creator support.

**Create High-Quality Content:**

Focus on creating valuable, engaging, and high-quality content that resonates with your target audience. Choose topics that you're knowledgeable and passionate about, and that have the potential to attract and retain viewers/readers.

Pay attention to content formats, such as video production quality, writing style, visual aesthetics, and storytelling techniques, to make your content more compelling and professional.

## Build Your Audience:

Consistently publish new content on your chosen platform to attract and retain viewers/readers. Establish a regular posting schedule to keep your audience engaged and coming back for more.

Promote your content through social media, email newsletters, online communities, and other channels to reach a wider audience and drive traffic to your platform.

Interact with your audience by responding to comments, messages, and feedback, and foster a sense of community around your content.

## Monetization Options:

**Advertising Revenue**: -

Platforms like YouTube and Medium offer advertising revenue-sharing programs that allow you to earn money based on the ads displayed on your content. - For YouTube, you can join the YouTube Partner Program (YPP) once you meet the eligibility requirements (generally, 1,000 subscribers and 4,000 watch hours in the past 12 months). - Medium offers the Partner Program, where writers can earn money based on member reading time and engagement with their articles.

**Sponsorships**: -

Collaborate with brands, companies, or other creators to sponsor your content. This could involve featuring sponsored products or services in your content, creating sponsored posts or videos, or promoting sponsored events or campaigns. - Negotiate sponsorship deals directly with brands or join influencer marketing platforms that connect creators with brands looking for sponsorship opportunities.

**Affiliate Marketing**: -

Promote products or services through affiliate marketing by including affiliate links in your content. You earn a commission for every sale or referral generated through your affiliate links. - Choose affiliate programs that are relevant to your niche and audience, and disclose your affiliate relationships transparently to maintain trust with your audience.

**Subscription/Membership Models**: -

Offer premium or exclusive content to your audience through subscription or membership models. Platforms like Patreon allow creators to offer subscription-based content and perks to their supporters in exchange for a monthly fee.

**Product Sales**: -

Sell digital or physical products related to your content niche. This could include eBooks, online courses, merchandise, artwork, or consulting services. - Use e-commerce platforms like Shopify, Gumroad, or WooCommerce to set up online stores and sell your products directly to your audience.

**Track and Analyze Performance**:

Monitor the performance of your content and monetization efforts using analytics tools provided by the platform or third-party services.

Track key metrics such as views, watch time, engagement, click-through rates, conversion rates, and revenue generated to understand what's working well and identify areas for improvement.

Use data-driven insights to optimize your content strategy, monetization tactics, and audience engagement efforts over time.

**Stay Compliant and Ethical**:

Familiarize yourself with the platform's content policies, community guidelines, and terms of service to ensure compliance and avoid violations that could jeopardize your monetization opportunities.

Maintain transparency and integrity in your content creation and monetization practices, and disclose any sponsored content, affiliate relationships, or potential conflicts of interest to your audience.

By consistently creating high-quality content, building a loyal audience, and leveraging various monetization methods, you can turn your passion for content creation into a profitable online venture. Keep experimenting, learning, and adapting to stay ahead in the ever-evolving landscape of online content creation and monetization.

# 4. Online Tutoring

If you have expertise in a particular subject, you can offer online tutoring services through platforms like Tutor.com, Chegg Tutors, or VIPKid.

Indeed, online tutoring is a popular way to make money online, especially if you have expertise in a particular subject. Here's a more detailed explanation of how you can get started with online tutoring through platforms like Tutor.com, Chegg Tutors, or VIPKid:

**Choose Your Platform**:

Research and choose a reputable online tutoring platform that aligns with your expertise, availability, and preferences. Some popular platforms include Tutor.com, Chegg Tutors, VIPKid, Wyzant, and Preply.

Consider factors such as the platform's user interface, tutoring subjects offered, payment structure, scheduling flexibility, and requirements for tutors.

**Complete the Application Process**:

Sign up for an account on the chosen platform and complete the application process to become a tutor.

Provide information about your educational background, teaching experience, areas of expertise, availability, and other relevant details.

Some platforms may require you to undergo background checks, verification of qualifications, or proficiency tests in your chosen subject areas.

### Create a Compelling Profile:

Build a comprehensive and compelling profile that highlights your qualifications, experience, teaching style, and areas of expertise.

Write a professional and engaging bio that introduces yourself to potential students and showcases your passion for teaching and helping others learn.

Upload relevant documents such as resumes, certificates, transcripts, or teaching credentials to verify your qualifications and expertise.

### Set Your Availability and Rates:

Determine your availability for tutoring sessions and set your preferred schedule on the platform.

Specify the subjects you're qualified to tutor in and set your tutoring rates or hourly fees based on your expertise, experience, and market rates.

Consider offering discounts or promotional rates for new students or recurring clients to attract more business.

### Promote Your Services:

Take proactive steps to promote your tutoring services and attract students to book sessions with you.

Optimize your profile with relevant keywords and tags to improve visibility in search results on the platform.

Participate in platform-specific marketing initiatives such as featured tutor listings, referral programs, or promotional campaigns.

Leverage social media, online forums, community groups, and other channels to reach out to potential students and promote your tutoring services.

## Deliver High-Quality Tutoring Sessions:

Prepare lesson plans, materials, and resources in advance to ensure a productive and engaging tutoring experience for your students.

Tailor your teaching approach to meet the individual learning needs, preferences, and goals of each student.

Use interactive teaching methods, multimedia resources, and real-life examples to reinforce concepts and facilitate understanding.

Provide constructive feedback, encouragement, and support to help students overcome challenges and achieve their academic objectives.

## Communicate Effectively:

Maintain clear and timely communication with your students regarding scheduling, session arrangements, lesson objectives, and progress tracking.

Respond promptly to student inquiries, messages, and feedback to address any concerns or questions they may have.

Foster a positive and supportive learning environment where students feel comfortable asking questions, sharing ideas, and expressing their learning needs.

## Collect Feedback and Reviews:

Encourage students to provide feedback and reviews of your tutoring sessions to build your reputation and credibility on the platform.

Use constructive feedback to identify areas for improvement and enhance the quality of your tutoring services over time.

Showcase positive testimonials and reviews on your profile to attract more students and increase your visibility as a top-rated tutor.

## Stay Updated and Adapt:

Stay informed about changes, updates, and trends in education, curriculum standards, teaching methodologies, and technological advancements relevant to your subject area.

Continuously seek opportunities for professional development, training, and skill enhancement to stay competitive and offer the best possible tutoring experience to your students.

Adapt your tutoring strategies, lesson plans, and teaching techniques based on feedback from students, evolving educational needs, and emerging trends in online learning.

By following these steps and consistently delivering high-quality tutoring services, you can build a successful online tutoring business and help students achieve their academic goals while earning a sustainable income from the comfort of your own home.

# 5. Sell Products Online

You can sell products without holding inventory by dropshipping through platforms like Shopify, Etsy, or Amazon. Alternatively, you can create and sell digital products like eBooks, courses, or printables.

## Dropshipping:

a. **Choose Your Platform**:

Sign up for an account on a dropshipping platform such as Shopify, WooCommerce (if using WordPress), Etsy, or Amazon.

Consider factors such as platform fees, ease of use, available features, and integrations with dropshipping suppliers.

b. **Find a Niche and Products**:

Research and identify a profitable niche market with high demand and low competition.

Select products to sell from reputable dropshipping suppliers or wholesalers. Look for products with good profit margins, reliable quality, and fast shipping times.

### c. Set Up Your Online Store:

Customize your online store with a professional design, branding elements, and product listings.

Create compelling product descriptions, images, and videos to showcase your products and attract customers.

Set up payment gateways, shipping options, and tax settings to facilitate transactions and ensure a seamless shopping experience for your customers.

### d. Market Your Products:

Implement marketing strategies to drive traffic to your online store and attract potential customers.

Use a combination of digital marketing tactics such as search engine optimization (SEO), social media marketing, email marketing, content marketing, influencer partnerships, and paid advertising to reach your target audience.

Leverage social proof, customer reviews, and testimonials to build trust and credibility with your audience.

### e. Process Orders and Fulfillment:

When a customer places an order on your online store, forward the order details to your dropshipping supplier.

Your dropshipping supplier will then fulfill the order by packaging and shipping the product directly to the customer on your behalf.

Keep track of order statuses, shipping updates, and customer inquiries to ensure smooth order processing and timely delivery.

f. **Customer Service and Support**:

Provide excellent customer service and support to address any questions, concerns, or issues raised by your customers.

Offer multiple channels for customer communication, such as live chat, email, phone support, and social media, to accommodate different preferences and needs.

Handle returns, exchanges, and refunds promptly and professionally to maintain customer satisfaction and loyalty.

g. **Optimize and Scale**:

Continuously monitor and analyze your store performance, sales metrics, and customer feedback to identify areas for improvement and optimization.

Experiment with different pricing strategies, product offerings, marketing campaigns, and sales tactics to maximize profitability and growth.

Scale your dropshipping business by expanding into new markets, adding more products to your catalog, or diversifying your sales channels.

## Sell Digital Products:

**Choose Your Product Type**:

Decide on the type of digital products you want to create and sell, such as eBooks, online courses, printables, templates, digital art, software, or digital downloads.

Identify a niche market or target audience for your digital products based on their interests, needs, and preferences.

b. **Create Your Product**:

Develop high-quality digital products that provide value and address specific pain points or problems faced by your target audience.

Use professional tools and software to create, design, and format your digital products, ensuring they are visually appealing, easy to use, and accessible to your customers.

c. **Set Up Your Online Store**:

Choose a platform or marketplace to sell your digital products, such as Shopify, Gumroad, Etsy, Teachable, Udemy, or Amazon Kindle Direct Publishing (KDP).

Create product listings with detailed descriptions, pricing, and images to showcase your digital products and attract customers.

d. **Market Your Products**:

Develop a marketing strategy to promote your digital products and reach your target audience effectively.

Utilize digital marketing channels such as social media, email marketing, content marketing, influencer partnerships, and paid advertising to drive traffic to your product listings.

Offer free samples, previews, or limited-time discounts to encourage potential customers to try your digital products and make a purchase.

e. **Deliver Your Products**:

Set up automated delivery systems or download links to deliver your digital products to customers instantly upon purchase.

Ensure a smooth and secure purchasing experience for your customers, with options for payment processing, digital downloads, and customer support.

### f. Provide Customer Support:

Offer customer support and assistance to help customers with any questions, issues, or technical problems they may encounter with your digital products.

Provide clear instructions, tutorials, and troubleshooting guides to help customers use and benefit from your digital products effectively.

### g. Optimize and Expand:

Monitor sales performance, customer feedback, and market trends to optimize your digital products and marketing strategies.

Experiment with pricing, packaging, bundling, and promotional offers to maximize sales and revenue.

Continuously update and improve your digital products based on customer feedback, technological advancements, and changes in market demand.

By leveraging dropshipping or creating and selling digital products online, you can build a profitable e-commerce business and generate passive income streams without the need for holding inventory or physical storefronts. With careful planning, execution, and ongoing optimization, you can create a successful online business that provides value to your customers and rewards you financially.

# 6. Affiliate Marketing

Promote products or services through affiliate marketing. You earn a commission for every sale or lead generated through your referral links. You can join affiliate programs of companies like Amazon Associates, ShareASale, or ClickBank.

**Choose Your Niche:**

Identify a niche market or industry that aligns with your interests, expertise, and target audience. Selecting a niche allows you to focus your efforts on promoting products or services that appeal to a specific audience.

**Research Affiliate Programs:**

Explore affiliate programs offered by companies, brands, or merchants within your chosen niche. Look for reputable affiliate networks or platforms that connect affiliates with advertisers and offer a wide range of products and services to promote.

Some popular affiliate networks and programs include Amazon Associates, ShareASale, ClickBank, CJ Affiliate (formerly Commission Junction), Rakuten Advertising (formerly LinkShare), and Impact.

### Join Affiliate Programs:

Sign up for affiliate programs that align with your niche and meet your criteria. Review the terms and conditions, commission rates, payment structure, cookie duration, and promotional resources offered by each affiliate program.

Complete the application process and provide any required information or documentation to become an approved affiliate.

### Select Products to Promote:

Choose products or services from the affiliate programs you've joined that are relevant to your audience and have the potential to generate sales or leads.

Consider factors such as product quality, brand reputation, customer demand, commission rates, and promotional materials available.

### Create Valuable Content:

Develop high-quality content that educates, entertains, or solves problems for your audience. This could include blog posts, articles, reviews, tutorials, videos, podcasts, social media posts, email newsletters, or other forms of content.

Incorporate affiliate links strategically within your content in a natural and non-intrusive way. Disclose your affiliate relationships transparently to your audience to maintain trust and credibility.

### Promote Your Affiliate Links:

Share your content and affiliate links across various online channels to reach your target audience and drive traffic to the products or services you're promoting.

Utilize digital marketing tactics such as search engine optimization (SEO), social media marketing, email marketing, content marketing, influencer partnerships, and paid advertising to amplify your promotional efforts.

Experiment with different promotional strategies, messaging, and channels to identify what works best for your audience and niche.

## Track Performance and Optimize:

Monitor the performance of your affiliate marketing campaigns using tracking tools and analytics provided by the affiliate programs or third-party platforms.

Track key metrics such as clicks, conversions, sales, leads, conversion rates, and earnings to assess the effectiveness of your promotional efforts.

Analyze data insights to identify top-performing products, traffic sources, and promotional strategies, and optimize your campaigns accordingly.

Test different variations of your content, affiliate links, calls-to-action, and promotional messages to improve conversion rates and maximize your affiliate earnings.

## Comply with Regulations:

Familiarize yourself with relevant regulations, laws, and guidelines governing affiliate marketing, advertising disclosures, and consumer protection in your jurisdiction.

Ensure compliance with affiliate program policies, Federal Trade Commission (FTC) guidelines, General Data Protection Regulation (GDPR) requirements, and other legal obligations related to affiliate marketing practices.

Clearly disclose your affiliate relationships, compensation arrangements, and potential biases to your audience in accordance with disclosure guidelines and best practices.

By following these steps and consistently delivering value to your audience through relevant and compelling content, you can build a successful affiliate marketing business and earn passive income by promoting products or services that resonate with your audience and drive conversions. With persistence, patience, and strategic execution, affiliate marketing can become a profitable revenue stream and a valuable asset in your online business portfolio.

# 7. Online Surveys and Market Research

Participate in online surveys or market research studies through platforms like Swagbucks, Survey Junkie, or Respondent to earn some extra cash.

**Choose Your Niche**:

Identify a niche market or industry that aligns with your interests, expertise, and target audience. Selecting a niche allows you to focus your efforts on promoting products or services that appeal to a specific audience.

**Research Affiliate Programs**:

Explore affiliate programs offered by companies, brands, or merchants within your chosen niche. Look for reputable affiliate networks or platforms that connect affiliates with advertisers and offer a wide range of products and services to promote.

Some popular affiliate networks and programs include Amazon Associates, ShareASale, ClickBank, CJ Affiliate (formerly Commission Junction), Rakuten Advertising (formerly LinkShare), and Impact.

**Join Affiliate Programs:**

Sign up for affiliate programs that align with your niche and meet your criteria. Review the terms and conditions, commission rates, payment structure, cookie duration, and promotional resources offered by each affiliate program.

Complete the application process and provide any required information or documentation to become an approved affiliate.

**Select Products to Promote:**

Choose products or services from the affiliate programs you've joined that are relevant to your audience and have the potential to generate sales or leads.

Consider factors such as product quality, brand reputation, customer demand, commission rates, and promotional materials available.

**Create Valuable Content:**

Develop high-quality content that educates, entertains, or solves problems for your audience. This could include blog posts, articles, reviews, tutorials, videos, podcasts, social media posts, email newsletters, or other forms of content.

Incorporate affiliate links strategically within your content in a natural and non-intrusive way. Disclose your affiliate relationships transparently to your audience to maintain trust and credibility.

## Promote Your Affiliate Links:

Share your content and affiliate links across various online channels to reach your target audience and drive traffic to the products or services you're promoting.

Utilize digital marketing tactics such as search engine optimization (SEO), social media marketing, email marketing, content marketing, influencer partnerships, and paid advertising to amplify your promotional efforts.

Experiment with different promotional strategies, messaging, and channels to identify what works best for your audience and niche.

## Track Performance and Optimize:

Monitor the performance of your affiliate marketing campaigns using tracking tools and analytics provided by the affiliate programs or third-party platforms.

Track key metrics such as clicks, conversions, sales, leads, conversion rates, and earnings to assess the effectiveness of your promotional efforts.

Analyze data insights to identify top-performing products, traffic sources, and promotional strategies, and optimize your campaigns accordingly.

Test different variations of your content, affiliate links, calls-to-action, and promotional messages to improve conversion rates and maximize your affiliate earnings.

## Comply with Regulations:

Familiarize yourself with relevant regulations, laws, and guidelines governing affiliate marketing, advertising disclosures, and consumer protection in your jurisdiction.

Ensure compliance with affiliate program policies, Federal Trade Commission (FTC) guidelines, General Data Protection Regulation (GDPR) requirements, and other legal obligations related to affiliate marketing practices.

Clearly disclose your affiliate relationships, compensation arrangements, and potential biases to your audience in accordance with disclosure guidelines and best practices.

By following these steps and consistently delivering value to your audience through relevant and compelling content, you can build a successful affiliate marketing business and earn passive income by promoting products or services that resonate with your audience and drive conversions. With persistence, patience, and strategic execution, affiliate marketing can become a profitable revenue stream and a valuable asset in your online business portfolio.

# 8. Virtual Assistant

Offer virtual assistant services to businesses or entrepreneurs who need help with administrative tasks, email management, scheduling, etc. Platforms like Upwork and Freelancer often have listings for virtual assistant positions.

**Choose Your Niche:**

Identify a niche market or industry that aligns with your interests, expertise, and target audience. Selecting a niche allows you to focus your efforts on promoting products or services that appeal to a specific audience.

**Research Affiliate Programs:**

Explore affiliate programs offered by companies, brands, or merchants within your chosen niche. Look for reputable affiliate networks or platforms that connect affiliates with advertisers and offer a wide range of products and services to promote.

Some popular affiliate networks and programs include Amazon Associates, ShareASale, ClickBank, CJ Affiliate (formerly Commission Junction), Rakuten Advertising (formerly LinkShare), and Impact.

## Join Affiliate Programs:

Sign up for affiliate programs that align with your niche and meet your criteria. Review the terms and conditions, commission rates, payment structure, cookie duration, and promotional resources offered by each affiliate program.

Complete the application process and provide any required information or documentation to become an approved affiliate.

## Select Products to Promote:

Choose products or services from the affiliate programs you've joined that are relevant to your audience and have the potential to generate sales or leads.

Consider factors such as product quality, brand reputation, customer demand, commission rates, and promotional materials available.

## Create Valuable Content:

Develop high-quality content that educates, entertains, or solves problems for your audience. This could include blog posts, articles, reviews, tutorials, videos, podcasts, social media posts, email newsletters, or other forms of content.

Incorporate affiliate links strategically within your content in a natural and non-intrusive way. Disclose your affiliate relationships transparently to your audience to maintain trust and credibility.

## Promote Your Affiliate Links:

Share your content and affiliate links across various online channels to reach your target audience and drive traffic to the products or services you're promoting.

Utilize digital marketing tactics such as search engine optimization (SEO), social media marketing, email marketing, content marketing, influencer partnerships, and paid advertising to amplify your promotional efforts.

Experiment with different promotional strategies, messaging, and channels to identify what works best for your audience and niche.

## Track Performance and Optimize:

Monitor the performance of your affiliate marketing campaigns using tracking tools and analytics provided by the affiliate programs or third-party platforms.

Track key metrics such as clicks, conversions, sales, leads, conversion rates, and earnings to assess the effectiveness of your promotional efforts.

Analyze data insights to identify top-performing products, traffic sources, and promotional strategies, and optimize your campaigns accordingly.

Test different variations of your content, affiliate links, calls-to-action, and promotional messages to improve conversion rates and maximize your affiliate earnings.

## Comply with Regulations:

Familiarize yourself with relevant regulations, laws, and guidelines governing affiliate marketing, advertising disclosures, and consumer protection in your jurisdiction.

Ensure compliance with affiliate program policies, Federal Trade Commission (FTC) guidelines, General Data Protection Regulation (GDPR) requirements, and other legal obligations related to affiliate marketing practices.

Clearly disclose your affiliate relationships, compensation arrangements, and potential biases to your audience in accordance with disclosure guidelines and best practices.

By following these steps and consistently delivering value to your audience through relevant and compelling content, you can build a successful affiliate marketing business and earn passive income by promoting products or services that resonate with your audience and drive conversions. With persistence, patience, and strategic execution, affiliate marketing can become a profitable revenue stream and a valuable asset in your online business portfolio.

# 9. Create an Online Course

If you have expertise in a particular area, you can create and sell online courses through platforms like Udemy, Teachable, or Skillshare.

Creating and selling online courses is an excellent way to monetize your expertise and share your knowledge with a global audience. Here's a detailed guide on how to create and sell an online course:

**Choose Your Topic**:

Identify a topic that you are knowledgeable and passionate about. Consider your expertise, experience, and what topics would resonate with your target audience.

Research market demand and competition to ensure there is an audience interested in your chosen topic.

**Define Your Audience**:

Determine who your target audience is for the course. Consider factors such as their demographics, interests, skill level, and learning goals.

Tailor your course content and marketing efforts to address the specific needs and preferences of your target audience.

**Outline Your Course Content:**

Create a detailed outline of the course content, including the main topics, subtopics, learning objectives, and key takeaways for each lesson.

Structure your course in a logical and sequential manner to facilitate learning and comprehension for your students.

**Create Course Materials:**

Develop high-quality course materials such as video lectures, presentations, written guides, worksheets, quizzes, assignments, and supplementary resources.

Use a combination of multimedia elements (e.g., text, images, videos, audio) to engage different learning styles and enhance the learning experience for your students.

**Choose a Platform:**

Select a platform to host and sell your online course. Popular options include Udemy, Teachable, Skillshare, Thinkific, Kajabi, and Coursera.

Evaluate factors such as platform features, pricing, course promotion tools, payment processing, student support, and terms of use to determine the best fit for your needs.

**Set Up Your Course:**

Create an instructor account on your chosen platform and set up your course profile.

Follow the platform's guidelines and requirements for course creation, including formatting specifications, file size limits, and quality standards.

Upload your course content, including video lectures, course materials, and supplementary resources, to the platform's course builder or content management system.

## Price Your Course:

Determine the pricing strategy for your course, considering factors such as the perceived value of the content, market demand, competition, and your own financial goals.

Choose between one-time payments, subscription models, or payment plans, and set the price accordingly.

Consider offering promotional discounts, coupons, or free trials to attract new students and encourage enrollment.

## Market Your Course:

Develop a marketing plan to promote your course and attract students. Utilize various channels such as social media, email marketing, content marketing, blogging, webinars, podcasts, guest appearances, and online communities.

Create compelling marketing materials such as course trailers, landing pages, promotional videos, testimonials, and case studies to showcase the value of your course and persuade potential students to enroll.

Leverage the marketing tools and features provided by the course platform to increase visibility, reach, and engagement with your target audience.

## Engage with Your Students:

Foster a supportive and interactive learning environment for your students by actively engaging with them throughout the course.

Encourage participation, discussion, and collaboration among students through forums, discussion boards, live Q&A sessions, office hours, and group activities.

Provide timely feedback, guidance, and support to help students overcome challenges, clarify concepts, and achieve their learning goals.

## Monitor Performance and Iterate:

Monitor the performance of your course, track key metrics such as enrollment, engagement, completion rates, student satisfaction, and revenue.

Analyze student feedback, reviews, and course evaluations to identify areas for improvement and iterate on your course content, structure, and delivery.

Continuously update and enhance your course based on student feedback, changes in industry trends, advancements in technology, and evolving learning needs to ensure its relevance and effectiveness over time.

By following these steps and creating a high-quality online course that delivers value and meets the needs of your target audience, you can build a successful online business and generate passive income from course sales. With dedication, creativity, and strategic planning, you can leverage your expertise to educate, inspire, and empower students around the world through your online course.

# 10. Freelance Writing

Offer your writing services to businesses, blogs, or publications. You can find writing gigs on platforms like Upwork, Freelancer, ProBlogger, or by directly pitching to websites and blogs.

Freelance writing is a flexible and rewarding way to make money online by leveraging your writing skills and expertise. Here's a detailed guide on how to get started as a freelance writer:

**Identify Your Niche and Expertise**:

Determine your areas of expertise, interests, and writing skills. Consider whether you have a specialization or niche that you're passionate about or have experience in, such as technology, finance, health, travel, lifestyle, or business.

Specializing in a niche can help you stand out from the competition and attract clients looking for writers with specific knowledge and expertise.

**Create a Portfolio**:

Compile a portfolio showcasing your best writing samples, articles, blog posts, case studies, whitepapers, or other relevant work. If you're just starting out and don't have published work, consider creating sample pieces that demonstrate your writing style, voice, and ability to engage readers.

Develop a professional writer's website or online portfolio to showcase your portfolio, writing services, testimonials, client list, and contact information. Use a clean and visually appealing design that highlights your writing skills and professionalism.

**Build Your Online Presence**:

Establish a strong online presence on professional networking sites like LinkedIn, as well as social media platforms such as Twitter, Facebook, and Instagram. Optimize your profiles to highlight your writing skills, expertise, and services.

Join online communities, forums, and groups relevant to your niche to network with other writers, editors, and potential clients. Participate in discussions, share valuable insights, and offer advice to establish yourself as a knowledgeable and helpful resource.

**Find Writing Gigs**:

Search for freelance writing opportunities on job boards, freelance marketplaces, and content platforms. Popular websites for finding writing gigs include Upwork, Freelancer, ProBlogger, Contena, BloggingPro, FlexJobs, and Mediabistro.

Browse job listings, writing gigs, and project opportunities based on your interests, skills, and preferences. Look for gigs that match your expertise and pay rates, and submit tailored proposals or pitches to potential clients.

Consider reaching out to websites, blogs, magazines, and businesses directly to pitch your writing services. Research their content, audience, and writing guidelines, and pitch unique and relevant story ideas or articles that align with their needs and interests.

## Pitch Your Services:

Craft personalized pitch emails or letters to introduce yourself to potential clients and pitch your writing services. Tailor your pitches to the needs, goals, and tone of each client or publication, and highlight how your writing skills and expertise can add value to their projects.

Keep your pitches concise, clear, and professional, focusing on the benefits and outcomes of working with you as a writer. Include links to your portfolio, relevant writing samples, and testimonials to support your pitch and demonstrate your credibility.

Follow up on your pitches after a reasonable period if you don't hear back, but avoid being overly persistent or spammy.

## Deliver High-Quality Work:

Once you secure writing gigs, deliver high-quality work that meets or exceeds your clients' expectations. Follow the project brief, style guidelines, and deadlines provided by the client, and communicate proactively if you have any questions or concerns.

Conduct thorough research, fact-checking, and editing to ensure accuracy, clarity, and professionalism in your writing. Tailor your writing style, tone, and voice to match the client's brand, audience, and objectives.

Be open to feedback, revisions, and constructive criticism from clients, and incorporate their input to improve your work and strengthen your client relationships.

## Manage Your Freelance Business:

Keep track of your writing projects, deadlines, payments, and client communications using project management tools, calendars, and invoicing software.

Set clear expectations with clients regarding payment terms, rates, project scope, revisions, and communication channels to avoid misunderstandings or disputes.

Stay organized and professional in your communications, invoices, contracts, and agreements with clients, and ensure you're complying with tax and legal requirements for freelance work in your jurisdiction.

## Build Long-Term Relationships:

Nurture and maintain relationships with your clients by providing exceptional service, delivering quality work consistently, and demonstrating reliability and professionalism.

Offer value-added services, such as content strategy, keyword research, SEO optimization, or social media promotion, to help clients achieve their content marketing goals and differentiate yourself from other freelance writers.

Seek opportunities for repeat business, referrals, and testimonials from satisfied clients, and prioritize building long-term partnerships that can lead to ongoing writing gigs and steady income.

By following these steps and proactively marketing your writing services, you can establish yourself as a successful freelance writer and build a sustainable career writing for businesses, websites, publications, and other clients. With dedication, persistence, and continuous improvement, you can turn your passion for writing into a profitable and fulfilling freelance business.

www.ingramcontent.com/pod-product-compliance
Lightning Source LLC
Chambersburg PA
CBHW081020240526
45471CB00018B/3915